Katy Simmons

Plays for the Period of Stagnation:
Lyudmila Petrushevskaya and the Theatre of
the Absurd

BIRMINGHAM SLAVONIC MONOGRAPHS NO.21

Katy Simmons

Plays for the Period of Stagnation:
Lyudmila Petrushevskaya and the Theatre of the Absurd

Published by the   Department of Russian Language and Literature
University of Birmingham
Edgbaston
Birmingham B15 2TT

© Series: University of Birmingham
© Contents No. 21 : Katy Simmons, 1992

ISBN   0 7044 1201 2
ISSN   0141-3805

Lyudmila Petrushevskaya's career as a playwright began at the age of thirty-five in 1973. She had already written many short stories,[1] but was inspired to write her first play, *Music Lessons* (*Uroki muzyki*), 'out of anger' at the lies she had heard praised as literature at a seminar with a successful author:

> He lied to sell his work. You can't sell inspiration but you can sell lies. I went home and immediately sat down to write, to explain how this happens in life. Then I forgot about my initial rage and only one thing remained: never, never, never to lie.[2]

From the outset, this insistence on never lying about contemporary life set Petrushevskaya at odds with officially sanctioned literature, which although permitted (and even encouraged) to pinpoint 'individual shortcomings and temporary difficulties', was still essentially as 'fundamentally optimistic' as Zhdanov had declared it to be at the First Congress of the Writers' Union in 1934. In contrast to this, Petrushevskaya's plays portray the material and spiritual poverty of Soviet society during the *period zastoya* (period of stagnation) without any *lakirovka* (glossing over). Unlike much popular and officially sanctioned Soviet literature of the 1970s (for example, such writers as Grekova, the latterly dissident Vladimov in *Three Minutes' Silence* (*Tri minuty molchaniya*), and members of the 'village prose' school, who portrayed a wholeness and community spirit in rural life perhaps more imagined than real)[3], Petrushevskaya's plays and short stories stress the absence of social cohesion rather than the sense of shared community, the *kollektivnoe nachalo*, which stands at the centre of Soviet life.

These plays touch relentlessly on many of the 'individual problems' that were still considered too problematic to be discussed in the '70s: alcoholism, domestic violence, lonely single mothers, absentee husbands, abortion, divorce, poverty and the housing shortage. The brutality of the plays' subject matter gives the lie to the cosy world of Socialist Realist theatre, with its inevitable happy endings, and for a long time only semi-professional and amateur studio theatres would stage them (in particular the *Chelovek* theatre-studio run by Alexei Arbuzov, with which Petrushevskaya is still connected). Yuri Lyubimov gave Petrushevskaya her first outing on the professional stage with *Love* (*Lyubov'*), staged as one of three one-act plays at the Taganka theatre

[1] See Wolfgang Kazak, *Entsiklopedicheskii slovar' russkoi literatury s 1917 goda*, London, 1988, 596-7.
[2] Interview with M. Zonina – 'Bessmertnaya lyubov' ', *Literaturnaya gazeta*, 47, 23 November 1983, 495.
[3] On this, see Katerina Clark 'The Centrality of Rural Themes in Postwar Soviet Fiction', in Geoffrey A. Hosking and George F. Cushing (eds.), *Perspectives on Literature and Society in Eastern and Western Europe*, London, 1989, 76-100.

from December 1980: and 1985 saw a production at Moscow's *Sovremennik* theatre of *Columbine's Flat (Kvartira Kolombiny)*, written four years earlier.[4]

However, the main premise of this study is that something other than their uncompromising nature made it well nigh impossible for Petrushevskaya's plays to be performed on the professional stage in the USSR until relatively recently, – that is, their extension beyond the boundaries of social criticism into the fringes of absurdity which brings into question the very philosophical foundations of Soviet society.

Martin Esslin, in his book *The Theatre of the Absurd*, remarks that after the rise and fall of Hitler, Absurdist drama struck a strong chord with German audiences who saw the ideology on which their society had been founded totally discredited, and identified with the loss of cohesion and meaning in the plays.[5]   By the 1970s a comparable situation existed in the USSR: the Soviet regime had been thoroughly discredited by years of illegality, revolutionary fervour had been replaced by economic torpor and ideological disaffection and no one could fail to notice the ever-widening gap between propaganda and reality.

Faith in Marxism-Leninism having fallen away, the cohesion of Soviet society had become a sham which made it fertile ground for absurdity: 'Absurd is that which is devoid of purpose... Cut off from his religious, metaphysical, and transcendental roots, man is lost: all his actions become senseless, absurd, useless'.[6]   Without faith in the Communist religion, the whole of Soviet life assumed the air of pointless farce that foreign visitors so often remarked upon, and writers outside the bounds of Socialist Realism were quick to portray Soviet life as a set of sham values and meaningless actions dictated from above, an illogical black joke directed at the people by the powers that be.[7]

However, it is not only the ridiculous side of the Absurd which Petrushevskaya's work reflects. As we shall see later, she shares the Absurdists' preoccupation with disintegration in a world which no longer has fixed values or the certainty that results from faith – the breakdown of society and human relations, and the disintegration of language as a means of communication between characters who are constantly affected by the passage of time and the destructive effects of external influences.

Of all the Western European Absurdists, Petrushevskaya's work is perhaps most similar to Harold Pinter's: both place their plays firmly in contemporary society, but neither can be described as a social realist, because the problems that they concern themselves with are not the

---

[4] See Alexander Gershkovich, *Teatr na Taganke – 1964-1984*, Benson, Vermont, 1986, 229;   and Kazak, 596-7.

[5] Martin Esslin, *The Theatre of the Absurd*, 3rd. edn., London, 1980, 295.

[6] Eugene Ionesco, 'Dans les armes de la Ville', quoted by Esslin, 23.

[7] For example Sorokin's *Ochered'*, Voinovich's *Ivan'kiada*.

soluble, inessential ones of everyday life, but questions of the survival of self, which Pinter describes as more real than social realism[8] with its didactic solutions: 'After the social realist has established the need for his reform, the basic problems of existence remain – loneliness, the impenetrable mystery of the universe, death'.[9] Likewise, Petrushevskaya refuses to give answers to questions: '... it's not the writer's place to answer questions. Our job is to *ask* them... so that other people start to think too. Each about himself. For me, a play begins when I realise that people will look for an answer to the questions it poses'.[10]

Both playwrights deal with characters ' "At the extreme edge of their living, where they are living pretty much alone" ',[11] facing the insoluble questions of life which society prefers to ignore by hiding behind routine and convention, and recognizing the basic absurdity of the human condition, that is, that the questions that really matter do not have solutions since man has lost faith in a god or a system that could be used to explain them. Like the characters in Pinter's and Beckett's plays, Petrushevskaya's characters (and through them her audience) are brought to the realization that their hopes and dreams are facile comforters used to block out the reality of man's incomprehension before the important, insoluble questions of existence: and facing this reality gives them new strength to live with life's absurdity:

> ... by facing up to anxiety and despair and the absence of divinely revealed alternatives, anxiety and despair can be overcome. The sense of loss at the disintegration of facile solutions and the disappearance of cherished illusions retains its sting only while the mind still clings to the illusions concerned. Once they are given up we have to readjust ourselves to the new situation and face reality itself. And because the illusions we suffered from made it more difficult for us to deal with reality, their loss will ultimately be felt as exhilarating. In the words of Democritus that Beckett is so fond of quoting, 'Nothing is more real than nothing'.[12]

The cathartic despair of this realization and the adoption of non-realist techniques that stress the breakdown of human communication, rather than the social criticism that they contain, have made the plays seem so harmful to Soviet society and set Petrushevskaya apart from other contemporary Soviet playwrights as a writer approaching the territory of the Absurd.

---

[8] Esslin, 263.
[9] Esslin, 263.
[10] Zonina, 495.
[11] Harold Pinter, interviewed by Kenneth Tynan, quoted by Esslin, 262.
[12] Esslin, 426.

4

Firmly rooted in modern Soviet society by their language and their settings, many of Petrushevskaya's plays are, superficially at least, indictments of the material conditions of life in the urban sprawl of contemporary Russia. They describe the cramped living quarters, the family squabbles, and the tension between generations forced to coexist in small flats and making ends meet on inadequate wages, pensions and maintenance payments. But their settings, as well as describing the material poverty and failure of Soviet society, are also indicative of the dislocation of human relations which underlies this failure – the absurdity of modern society, deprived of faith or a sense of belonging. This society is described as follows by Albert Camus in *The Myth of Sisyphus*:

> A world that can be explained by reasoning, however faulty, is a familiar world. But in a universe that is suddenly deprived of illusions and of light man feels a stranger. He is an irremediable exile, because he is deprived of memories of a lost homeland as much as he lacks the hope of a promised land to come. This divorce between man and his life, the actor and his setting, truly constitutes the feeling of Absurdity.[13]

This sense of isolation and alienation from one's surroundings permeates Petrushevskaya's plays. Many have no stage directions as to their setting, which can only be guessed at from the dialogue: some, as they gradually unfold, reveal to what extent they are cut off from humanity and humane values – *The Execution* (*Kazn'*) takes place on death row; the *Isolation Ward* (*Izolirovannyi boks*) of one play's title is not simply an isolation ward, but one where patients are sent to die –

> B: Well, it's an isolation ward. An isolation ward for us. So as not to frighten them. We're in a good hospital. They don't want to frighten people. (238, *Pesni*)[14]

These settings are inescapable; like those of Pinter's plays, they denote the edge of human experience, where characters are alone with their consciences and must face reality.

Other plays express the breakdown of human contact through their setting: *A House and a Tree* (*Dom i derevo*) finds a father and son on opposite sides of the gate leading to the father's house, which is locked and wired up to a burglar alarm – father and son are symbolically separated as they are separated by their different philosophies of life. *The Stairwell* (*Lestnichnaya kletka*) takes place in the stairwell of the

---

[13] Quoted by Esslin, 23.
[14] Two collections of Petrushevskaya's plays have been published: *Pesni XX veka*, M., 1988 and *Tri devushki v golubom*, M., 1989. Page references are to the later volume, unless marked (*Pesni*).

block of flats where a woman lives alone behind a padded door and refuses entry to the only people who are honest with her or show her any sympathy, two musicians from a funeral orchestra whom she has met while seeking a husband with the aid of a matchmaker.

The stairwell is also perhaps symbolic of the depths to which humanity – and in particular its male half – has sunk; the two musicians, Slava and Yura, drink with no thought of tomorrow, trying to dull the pain of existence, and admit that 'down in the entrance hall – that's the only place for us' (214). They, like the three male friends who meet together in *Cinzano* (*Chinzano*) in an isolated flat, in a *'bare room'* with *'two chairs picked up from the dump, a park bench, a cardboard box that once contained sweets'* (107) have no place in their homes and spend their time escaping from normal human relationships in nondescript drinking hide-outs, ignoring their responsibilities to their children, wives and parents.

The decay of human relations is perhaps best typified in the setting of *Three Girls in Blue* (*Tri devushki v golubom*), where three distant relatives are forced to flee from one leaking-roofed room to another of the dacha that they are all trying to claim possession of, 'like refugees' (177), constantly arguing over who is to blame for the rotting roof and all denying responsibility for the repairs.

In contrast to these decaying settings, some (but only a very small number) of Petrushevskaya's characters live in comparative luxury, but are spiritually no better off. To those who have it, the importance of material wealth overrides their personal relationships and the connotations of affluence are invariably negative in these plays: the possession of a Zhiguli car, the acme of Soviet material desires, is at several points connected with criminality, as in *Three Girls in Blue,* or a love of things which obscures affection for people, as in *I'm a Sweden Fan (Ya boleyu za Shvetsiyu)* and *A House and a Tree.* Nikolai Ivanovich, the well-heeled bureaucrat with whom the desperate Ira has an affair in *Three Girls in Blue*, tries to impress her by repeatedly mentioning all the things he owns and his trips abroad: when she is finally enticed back to his Moscow flat he makes these offers to her –

> Nikolai Ivanovich: Come on, eat. Would you like pineapple in its own juice? Something else? Granulated Nestlé coffee... Should I make you a caviar sandwich?...Or some port, perhaps? I'll pour you some – it's genuine Portuguese....(179)

Offering her things – food, drink, her taxi fare home – is his expression of devotion to her: what Ira *wants* is affection, in her past there are already too many men who have paid the taxi fare home until she has realized that it might just as well be her price. She finds herself surrounded by objects, which seem to proliferate – his wife's three shower caps, the photos of his teenage daughter that cover the walls, all of which serve to remind her that she has no place in the comfortable, bourgeois world in which things rather than emotions are the currency of human exchange.

Likewise the Kozlov family in *Music Lesssons* have '*carpets, crystal, polished furniture*' (9) while their neighbours the Gavrilovs live in a flat which is '*clean and tidy, but the stamp of hardship is visible on everything*' (6). However, the bourgeois Kozlovs find no comfort in their wealth: the arrival of their son's mercenary girlfriend, Nadya, threatens them, and the music lessons which their son Nikolai took as a child, the symbol of all the family's betterment, are rejected by him on his return from the army as an endless embarrassment. The family's comparative wealth and the offers that they make their son of a co-operative flat and a car if he marries a suitable girl are only a cover; material success conceals a failed marriage, and parents who, in 'wanting the best' for their son, have always been pursuing their own goals rather than considering what he might want (Kozlov senior describes his son's music lessons as 'six years of *my life*' (9) (– my italics)).

The only point that the Gavrilovs and the Kozlovs have in common is the televison set that blares in the corner of both their flats throughout the play, and seems to hold both families in thrall. It has the power to intrude on any conversation, speakers concentrating more on the screen than on what they themselves are saying: '*continuous explosions can be heard from the television. Anna Stepanovna waits until a respite in the battle, then hurriedly finishes her story*' (8). At times both families turn and sit silent, as though entranced by what is happening on the screen (invisible to the audience, who hear only a soundtrack which conveys no sense): it has become the pivot and the ruler of family life and they turn to it rather than to each other, the well off and the materially dispossessed equally unable to establish communication in a world seemingly taken over by mass communication without meaning.

The 'divorce between man and his life' expressed in the play's settings is intensified in the central theme of the decay of home and family which runs through almost all of Petrushevskaya's plays. These are traditionally the linchpins of society, the co-ordinates by which man finds his bearings in life, and their disintegration marks man's loss of roots in modern society, a homelessness which is spiritual as much as it is actual in contemporary life, as exemplified in the monologue *Songs of the Twentieth Century* (*Pesni XX veka*). (Harold Pinter, incidentally, shares this preoccupation with '... a room of one's own as a symbol for one's place in the world'.)[15] A young man, living alone on the rented veranda of an isolated house, uses his tape recorder to record 'all the songs of the twentieth century' (183, *Pesni*), which include quotations

---

[15] Esslin, 247.

half-remembered from Esenin, sentimental songs and Socialist Realist clichés, phrases repeated from television and radio broadcasts and even the recorded warnings to passengers played on Moscow buses. There is no constant theme and nothing to believe in; the songs of the twentieth century do not include hymns.

A phrase repeatedly heard in these plays is 'I've nowhere to go', as characters move from rented verandas and partitioned corners to entrance halls and finally on to the streets, the prospect of a home of one's own continually receding. Au, a character in the farcical *Andante,* is thrown out by her husband whilst she is in hospital miscarrying their child; then the owners of the flat she has rented come back to reclaim it, and she is reduced to begging them to allow her to sleep on the floor in the kitchen, the bathroom or, as she loses her battle, even in the hallway.

This sense of dispossession is what lies at the heart of *Three Girls in Blue,* a play in which the characters are in part parodies of those in Chekhov's *Three Sisters (Tri sestry).* But while Chekhov's sisters are only gradually pushed out of their home as the play progresses, Petrushevskaya's three girls start off on the veranda or in decrepit rooms unusable in wet weather. The house is not theirs – they rent rooms at prices they do not know how they afford from the aging Fedorovna, but the owner is a distant relative, living out her days in an old people's home in Drezna. Not being sure who stands to inherit the house, none of the girls is willing to repair it, so half the roof has gradually rotted away: 'a house without a master soon decays' (149).

The same formula could apply to their family relations, which seem tenuous to say the least. Two of the girls, Ira and Tat'yana, are bringing up their children alone, the third, Svetlana, is still married to the alcoholic Valera, who puts in the occasional appearance. Old Fedorovna declares that she never loved, and quickly left, her husband and does not know where he is buried, neglected her son when he was a child and is in turn being neglected by him and his wife in her old age. What brings them all together is even more questionable: the explanation of the girls' kinship (which seems to be one common great grandmother and great grandfather) is confused and contradictory. Nobody knows all the details, some branches of the family seem to be irredeemably lost and the names that each girl remembers are different and seemingly unconnected: this familial decay is further symbolized by the girls' confusion between the words *pometa* (mark, note) and *pomet* (litter, brood or dung)(147).

These are not Chekhov's almost telepathically close sisters – instead they argue and misunderstand each other constantly:

> Svetlana: But we're *sisters*! Well, let's drink to our acquaintance.
> ...

> Tat'yana: We're (*she hesitates*) second cousins.
> Valera: You've got to drink. So as not to go under.(151)

Ira, the play's central figure, perhaps expresses best the dispossession, the sense of being *lishnii* (superfluous) that has haunted Russian literature for so long:

> Ira: Tanechka, how do you live when you're completely alone on this earth, when absolutely nobody needs you.... I've never had a sister or a brother.
> Tat'yana: But you have a mother.
> Ira: She's no mother... my mother hates me. She doesn't love me.
> (156)

She becomes progressively more placeless as the play unfolds; – a teacher of obscure and marginal languages (Welsh, Cornish and Manx), she is from the start the other girls' victim, at the dacha only because she cannot stand spending the summer with her censorious mother. Attempting to escape her life she becomes Nikolai Ivanovich's lover, only to find herself first in his flat full of reminders of his wife and daughter, then, when she follows him to Koktebel, rejected by him and threatened with being thrown off the beach where he is relaxing with his family. Finally, needing desperately to return to Moscow, where her son has been abandoned by his grandmother, she is reduced to begging, hysterical, on the airport floor to be given a ticket: her family has fallen apart, she has lost her one, illusory, chance of love, and finally she loses all human dignity. At this point, Ira disappears from the stage and we hear only her disembodied desperate voice, so little of her humanity remains.

When she returns to the dacha at the end of the play, Ira is calm, accepts the other two girls' demands, and even smiles and laughs as she never previously has. The depth of her despair and isolation have been cathartic for her and compelled her to face the reality of her life –' "... for a moment the *boredom of living* is replaced by the *suffering of being*" '[16] – she has come to realize that 'nothing is more real than nothing', and having faced the depths of the human condition, and forsaken the illusion she had of happiness, she can accept life without dreams and live with her reality.

The isolation which Ira experiences, the true human condition, is approached in almost all the plays through the collapse of the bonds by which man usually tries to escape loneliness, the family ties which, by convention, hold society together. Any real love in these plays is almost unbargained for ('You've unexpectedly turned out to be a good man' (183), Ira tells Nikolai Ivanovich in *Three Girls in Blue,* when still

---

[16] Samuel Beckett, *Proust*, quoted by Esslin, 59. Esslin's italics.

duped by his attentions), and more usually absent from marriages. The ironically named *Love* portrays a couple, Sveta and Tolya, on their return from their registry office wedding. They are lonely people, marrying to escape their loneliness, and hardly really know each other. Tolya readily admits that he has married Sveta without love –

> Tolya: I can't love. Whatever you do to me. I'm not capable of it. I'm a moral cripple in that respect. I'm not capable of it. I've told you that. (220)

But after going through a large *kandidatura* (candidature, list) of prospective wives, he decides on Sveta –

> Tolya: At first I just felt nothing towards you, a regular calm feeling, but then, turning everything over in my mind, I gradually began to realize that that calm, regular feeling must mean something. I mean that that nothing is the most precious thing, the thing I need more than any other relationship. (222)

Love is reduced to 'nothing', the ultimate expression of Tolya's failure to find his place in humanity –

> A great deal lies behind that 'nothing'– an utter lack of emotional good breeding, underdeveloped feelings, fear of loneliness, acute mental pain and at the same time – simple-minded insensitivity. Their mutual alienation threatens to grow into the vindictiveness which characterizes almost all the relationships between the characters in these plays....[17]

Despite this, they stay together, preferring their acknowledged mutual indifference to the loneliness which it replaces: having spoken the truth about their (lack of) emotion for each other, they leave to face their reality without any illusion of love.

Violence, as Elena Gessen points out, is inherent in almost all the relationships in Petrushevskaya's plays, lying just below the surface of 'civilized' family life. The doting father of *Music lessons* used to beat his son when he was small:

> Nikolai: You used to give me the strap for lying.
> Fedor Ivanovich: Exactly.
> Nikolai: And because of that, I learnt how to lie properly, so that you wouldn't find out... (62)

---

[17] Elena Gessen, 'Kto boitsya Lyudmily Petrushevskoi?', *Vremya i my*, 1984, 81, 115.

The lie of the happy family, underpinned by violence, is paralleled by the false morality this violence has taught Nikolai. In *The Uncooked Joint, or a Friends' Meeting* (*Syraya noga, ili vstrecha druzei*), a confused party comes to an end when Serezha, seemingly inevitably, beats up his wife, Natasha –

> Natasha: I'll explain everything now. Only don't hit me.
> Serezha: Not hit you? *How can I not hit you?* (101) (my italics)

Their 'friends' hurry away, ignoring what has happened; their indifference to Serezha's brutality is quite terrifying.

The collapse of the family seems to be taken for granted, especially by men, most of whom appear totally isolated, both from their families and from their own emotions. Yura, the roving musician of *The Stairwell*, readily admits to Galya men's faithlessness and pronounces the family dead:

> Yura: Oh, don't trust us, don't trust us blokes. You think we need that kind of burden [marriage]? We just want to have fun and spend a bit of time pleasantly, like a man can do with a woman. What do we need from all these extra complications and hasty marriages?
> ...
>
> Yura: So, you see how it is, Galya?
> Galya: No, how is it?
> Yura: In this day and age, the family no longer exists.
> Galya: So what is there?
> Yura: (*Philosophically*) There's only a tribe of females with their young, and lone males. (210/211)

Two one-act plays, *Cinzano* and *Smirnova's Birthday* (*Den' rozhdeniya Smirnovoi*), the former featuring three men, the latter three women who know them, portray the emotional divide that exists between the sexes. The three men, old drinking friends, are strangers in their own families and maintain the minimum contact with them. They express only the scantest feelings of obligation to their children or their parents. Pasha has bought his mother some flowers – to Valya's disgust:

> Valya: Why've you bought flowers for your mother? Parents don't need much, only that their beloved son should come round to see them, have a bite to eat, sit there under their loving gaze....I don't take my mother flowers. No, I turn up there myself. I mean more to her than flowers. While they're still alive, I feel I'm obliged to go and see them... (122)

What Valya does not know is that Pasha's mother has died; the flowers are for her funeral, which he should be organizing rather than drinking with his friends.

By contrast, Smirnova and her friends show remarkable – perhaps desperate – faith in the family as the only thing that holds their lives together: their talk turns instinctively to their families and the problems of keeping going when husbands desert their children and parents gradually lose health and the ability to look after grandchildren. Polina, the wife of Kostya, the most dissolute and indifferent of the men, loves him despite the obvious breakdown in their relations, and refuses even to consider leaving him. She stresses the solidity of her family's past, the wars it has survived with the symbols of family tenacity intact, her inherited Singer sewing machine and Underwood typewriter, from an age of greater certainty, before the onslaught of the twentieth century: and she holds out hope for its continued survival through her daughter:

> Polina. Yes, it's a good thing to have a daughter, you can pass all your valuables to her, not to some unknown daughter-in-law. (134)

Polina clings to the idea of the family, which acts as her anchor, despite her husband having clearly opted out of all family ties.

The cornerstone of Polina's faith is her children, and the same applies to almost all the women in Petrushevskaya's plays: 'we live for the sake of our children' (137), Polina insists, and Rita agrees, having herself had a child although the father was against it and left her before it was born. Even the faithless Elya Smirnova, who tells Polina the truth about Kostya's indifference, cannot deny her regret at having lacked the courage to become a mother, in spite of her circumstances:

> Elya.... Do you think it's any fun being a single mother with a kid whose father's twelve years younger than you and who doesn't even want to recognize his child, and with absolutely no prospects? Do you think that would be any fun for a little kid... my little one... What have I done, oh, what have I done... (138)

Mothers in these plays love their children militantly: in *Visiting Time* (*Svidanie*), for example, the mother of a multiple murderer refuses to believe his guilt, seeing him as a sick child, a persecuted innocent who should be protected rather than executed –

> Mother.... He's ill, for God's sake, he can't answer for his own actions. He's tortured by his thoughts. I don't know what you're thinking of, shooting sick men. Let's go home, let's go, I'll put you to bed. Let's go; I'll take you away...that's right, quietly now (*Looks towards the guard*) It's not allowed? But he's ill. He's out

of his mind. (*Looks at the guard*) I can't take him? Don't cry, my love, you're not well. They'll give you a doctor's certificate. (223, *Pesni*).

Notwithstanding the mothers' great love, all readily agree that bringing up children is *katorga* (hard labour); they play cruel practical jokes, deliberately hurt each other and tell lies, and will eventually abandon their parents to a lonely old age. One group of plays, *Grandma Blues (Babulya-blyus)*, concentrates on the theme of desertion and the isolation so feared by the old. *I'm a Sweden Fan* depicts a stepmother and stepson, after the death of the boy's father. The boy's maternal grandmother suddenly appears, not having seen him since his natural mother's death; she has no one in the world except the grandson she has neglected, and tries to buy his affections. His stepmother too is desperate for his company, threatening to kill herself if he leaves: he remains unmoved by either of them – his school friends and the football match on the television mean more to him than the women's suffering.

The old face their children's desertion as a matter of course: Anchutka, heroine of *Get Up, Anchutka! (Vstavai, Anchutka!)*, greets each day thus:

> Anchutka: Every morning I get up and face life. Anchutka, I say, get up! *Nobody's going to get up for you!* (260) (my italics)

The older patient in the *Isolation Ward*, A., sees no reason to live, understanding full well that she is only a burden to her grown-up daughter, and a reminder of her dead granddaughter, standing in the way of the new life her daughter must build to escape her loss:

> B: What do I need even another day or two for? Marusya [her daughter] doesn't need me, I'll clear out and she can bring whoever she wants round. She can build herself a new life, have a little baby. Then she'll forget about me altogether, me and little Irena [her dead granddaughter], we'll be thrown aside. (235, *Pesni*)

The cruelty inherent in parents' desertion by their children is no more than repayment for the cruelty meted out by the parents – the beatings and the emotional neglect that fill childhood in these plays – and reflects the contradictory nature of the relationship between parents and offspring, which, as the character M. points out in *A Glass of Water (Stakan vody)*, can mean either murder or a glass of water as comfort in their old age for parents (282). *Three Girls in Blue* exemplifies the tortuous nature of parent/child ties, based as it is around the relationships of three mothers (and daughters in their own right). Each declares her devotion for her son – but exclusively for her own son, who in her eyes can do no wrong – although all three boys appear to be equally vicious. Tat'yana also sings the praises of motherhood –

> Tat'yana: Mama! The first word we all say, and the last. Our mothers give birth to us in torment, bring us up, feed us. What else? They do our laundry. Everything we're doing now. And they work too. (156/157)

Ira's only response is that *her* mother hates her, which would seem to be true from the things her mother says about her on the phone to friends – that she never comes home, and neglects her mother. Yet when Ira does arrive home, in the middle of a phone conversation, her mother's reaction is quite different; although ignoring her daughter, she tells her interlocutor ' I'm quite simply laughing from happiness (*she wipes away a tear*)' (175). 'Laughter through tears' seems to be an appropriate description of this relationship in which both partners love and need each other so much, but are at the same time equally determined to inflict hurt on each other and prove their independence. In *Love*, Sveta's decision to stay with Tolya is prompted by the arrival of her mother, who wants to deprive Sveta of the companionship, if not the happiness, of marriage as she herself has been deprived of it for thirty years, and force her daughter to stay with her.

The failure of humanity to maintain contact with even those who should be closest, and the sado-masochism of the one relationship which seems to be just about surviving – the death of the family as a foundation of human relations – stands as a metaphor for the loss of fixed values according to which society can function, and man's failure to communicate, and perhaps even failure to recognize, his own emotions. The collapse of the family is symbolic of a wider collapse of human values, and an ignorance of moral or humane values. Elena Gessen remarks of the characters who people these plays:

> Petrushevskaya as a rule portrays that stratum of society which someone neatly described as the 'lumpen-intelligentsia'; her characters often have academic degrees and even attain the heights of fame in life. Their lumpenness comes from their utter moral deafness, their total lack of any moral orientation whatsoever. Sympathy, charity, compassion – these words do not exist in their vocabulary: love has been replaced by cohabitation: instead of friends they have drinking pals.[18]

Isaiah Berlin describes the Russian intelligentsia as '... a movement of educated, morally sensitive Russians...They believed in personal and

---

[18] Elena Gessen, 'Pobeg iz sotsrealizma, ili drugaya proza?', *Strana i mir*, Nov/Dec 1989, 6[54], 177.

political liberty, in the removal of irrational social inequalities and in truth...' and the 'Soviet intelligentsia' as a misnomer for educated professionals who have, however, lost '... the moral character, the intellectual integrity, the sensitive imagination and immense human attractiveness of the old intelligentsia.'[19]

This new 'intelligentsia' is the one which peoples *Cinzano,* people who, from their behaviour and drinking habits, one would not expect to be responsible Soviet citizens, scientists in research institutes who have the opportunity of travelling abroad. They have been robbed of all humanity by drink, which has become their *raison d'être*, an end in itself, for which they express more love than for their wives:

> Valya: Why escape from reality, if the reality of the situation is simply that we love to drink, we love this business, and not out of any highfalutin notion of forgetting. Why hide behind fancy phrases all the time? We drink for the love of drinking. But we're still forced to justify our little party. Whose business is it? Who do we have to justify ourselves to? (114)

One of their women friends is also said to drink 'because of her circumstances' (119). Valya rejects this reason – 'She wants to drink, so she does.' (119) She too is a *kandidat nauk* (roughly the equivalent of a British M.Sc.).

As a result of his drinking, Kostya has been diagnosed as having 'dysfunction'–

> Valya: Of the intestines?
> Kolya: No, of everything... *Dysfunction of the organism.*(119) (my italics)

His dispossession and indifference are such that he is no longer a functioning human being, his only emotions comical drunken affection and aggression; he is sinking, and does not even see his descent as such:

> Kostya: ...but I'm not sinking, I'm living. The kids are fed, clothed, shod, the TV works... (117)

Only Pasha can still possibly escape complete disengagement from humanity: his mother has died and he knows that he should be making funeral arrangements rather than sitting drinking. At first he tries to ignore this, saying his mother is having an operation tomorrow, and that 'everything'll be OK' (116). But he knows that this is a lie, and

19 Isaiah Berlin, 'The State of Europe: Christmas Eve, 1989', *Granta*, Winter 1990, 30, 149-50.

keeps insisting that he *must* leave, *must* hurry, that he cannot miss the last bus – he must not be late, for he knows that this is his last chance to prove himself human: but the others think he is joking. Kostya finds Pasha's mother's dress and slippers and dresses up in them, and impresses his own indifference on Pasha –

> Kostya: It's not time for you to go anywhere. You don't have to do anything for anyone...Above all, don't think. It never happens, you can't *be* definitively late. (122)

But Pasha is 'definitively late'; he keeps on drinking until he goes blind and convinces himself that there is no need to hurry, he can go tomorrow – but as tomorrow is Saturday, there is no need to go then either. As the play ends, Pasha is asking Kostya to stay with him until Sunday.

> Pasha: But you'll stay with me 'til Sunday. You gave me your word. (123)

The word of his drinking pal has come to mean more for Pasha than the commitments that he has to his own mother, and it is tempting to think that they will be together not only *do voskresen'ya* (until Sunday), but *do voskreseniya* (until Judgement Day), two lost alcoholic souls in the limbo of their featureless drinking den.

Yura and Slava in *The Stairwell* are two more shameless drunks with seemingly similar motivation to Kostya; but they differ in one point – they are entirely truthful, to themselves and to Galya. They happily admit their own faithlessness and, rather than hiding in the bottle, face the human condition with equanimity – both are musicians in a funeral band, and death is literally a day-to-day affair for them:

> Slava: ...You have each day and you have to live through it in such a way that it's not incredibly painful. And it can be agonizingly good. And so, day in day out. It's all the same, nothing lasts. Live for the day and be happy for the day. Why look to the future? You know what lies ahead for all of us? The sum total – Chopin's *March* at the most. And they *might* not order that for you. And yet there's no one who loves life more than us...(212/213)

Galya has constructed a neat life to keep desperation at bay:

> Galya: It's OK by me living alone. I get home from work, I've a nice clean flat, my TV, a chest of drawers, everything I need. I was so pleased when they gave me this flat. Mum and Dad had

quarrelled and fought so much of late. It was a relief for me! I've got some peace at last! (210)

– but her peace and quiet conceals the fact that her father eloped with her best friend, and her mother tried to commit suicide and now refuses to live with the daughter whom she considers a traitor. The arrival of Yura and Slava intrudes the painful truth into this peace and quiet, and something happens between Galya and Yura ('(*something happens between Galya and Yura at this moment; their intonation changes*)' (207)) – they almost make contact; Yura's dire warnings about male nature are made not maliciously, hoping to destroy Galya's dreams, but to save her from the fate of a loveless marriage; and instead of sending them away, Galya feeds the two men and gives them a bottle of vodka – but asks them to go downstairs, away from her door, to drink it. They come so close to understanding and actually feeling emotion for each other (pity, even love, maybe), but fall victim to man's inability to communicate truly, which Beckett described in his essay on Proust:

> ... if love... is a function of man's sadness, friendship is a function of his cowardice; and if neither can be realised because of the impenetrability (isolation) of all that is not "cosa mentale", at least the failure to possess may have the nobility of that which is tragic, whereas the attempt to communicate where no communication is possible is merely a simian vulgarity, or horribly comic, like the madness that holds a conversation with the furniture.[20]

Galya, an almost tragic figure, returns to her empty flat; Yura becomes once again Slava's clowning partner and the two depart to drink their bottle in some seedy entrance hall.

The tragic and the comic failure of human communication plays a role in all of Petrushevskaya's plays, and is part of a wider complete breakdown of society, deprived of moral or religious laws to hold it together: in the farcical *Andante,* a family of diplomats speak a different, incomprehensible language to the homeless woman they want to throw out of their flat; in the almost-tragic *Music Lessons* two girls become the victims of Nikolai's ability to tell lies and his parents' heartless bourgeois morality which allows them to insist self-righteously that they are willing to help anybody less fortunate than themselves, but turn away their own illegitimate grandson. Brutality is everyday – from the neighbours in *Three Girls in Blue,* who shoot dogs at random and themselves die just as randomly, drowning while drunk, to the prison guards in *The Execution*, who worry not about killing the prisoner, but about whether they have been professionally trained for the job. This society is falling apart, from the houses that form its material fabric to

---

[20] Quoted in Esslin, 32.

the conventions of morality and social co-operation that hold human relationships together.

This social decay is revealed with a brutality that suits it well – the ' ... brutal refusal to compromise, the brutality and accuracy of her way of seeing, stripped of all illusions'[21] that is Petrushevskaya's trademark and one of the reasons that her plays remained for so long unperformed in the Soviet Union. Like Beckett, whose 'whole work is an endeavour to name the unnameable',[22] Petrushevskaya determinedly speaks the truth about life, and places her characters (and her audience) in situations where they are brought to question the validity of the life they are living:

> I was already over twenty-five when I began to write [– stories, I mean]. They weren't particularly wise, but I piled up a lot of questions, like: why? What right do they have? Not 'who's to blame?' but 'why?' *Why do people, knowing all they do, live like that all the same*? (my italics)[23]

Each of these plays brings characters to the edge of their existence, the point where they meet reality, Democritus's most real 'nothing', Tolya's 'nothing' in *Love*. Some , like Ira in *Three Girls in Blue*, break away from their former illusions and accept 'nothing', given the opportunity to try to start again without self-delusion. Some, like Nikolai in *Music Lessons*, fail when faced with nothing. He realizes the emptiness of his parents' marriage and the moral code by which they have brought him up and the hypocrisy of their behaviour in rejecting his calculating, pushy girlfriend Nadya and trying to force him into marrying their 'poor but honest' neighbour, Nina Gavrilova: it even seems as though he will reject them entirely and take responsibility for Nadya and their child. But it turns out that this behaviour is a joke to annoy his parents – in fact he understands as well as his father that ' ... we're Kozlovs, do you understand what that means? We'll do anything for our own family, for our own kind' (67). He turns away from nothing, and sits down to watch TV with his parents, ignoring the plight of the two girls he has deserted.

V. Malinkovich remarks on the *bogoostavlennost'* (desertion by God) and *bezottsovshchina* (fatherlessness) of Petrushevskaya's characters[24] – their sense of desertion and isolation – and points out the similarity between Ivan Karamazov's rejection of God and realization that without God everything is possible and phrases used in *Three Girls in Blue*:

---

[21] Gessen, *Strana i mir*, 177.

[22] Esslin, 86.

[23] Zonina, 495.

[24] Vladimir Malinkovich, 'Sostradanie (o p'esakh L. Petrushevskoi)', *Forum*, 1987, 16, 202.

Svetlana: What I wouldn't do for the tears of a child.(162)
...

Svetlana: Oh God, when they haven't got a father, everyone can do as they like. (164)

He contends however that this appeal to God and recognition of *bogoostavlennost'* means that the characters are not, unlike Karamazov, entirely lost, and can still be saved by love for their children, love based on sacrifice. Indeed Petrushevskaya has said that perhaps there is a 'grain of salvation' in her writing – '... Why *do* people tell each other stories? So as to try and escape from their burden. So as to maintain in themselves a sense of the ideal, of what ought to be'.[25]

But it seems that this ideal love remains ideal, rather than becoming reality in these plays, and perfect love between mother and child becomes no more possible. Petrushevskaya would like to believe in the power of love, but the reality of both children and parents – the truth she insists on – keeps encroaching on this belief and the plays express more fully the faithlessness of this age than the redeeming love that always remains ambiguous. Like Beckett, Petrushevskaya has a deep sympathy for humanity facing the ineffabilty of existence: 'my stories ask: can one really live that way? And the sensitive reader will answer: no. His task then is to discover how to live differently...*The task is to remain humane under all circumstances*' (my italics).[26] But in a world without faith, a world deserted by God and gradually falling apart, the truthful observer cannot but see the ridiculous – the absurd – nature of man's attempts to live and escape the emptiness of reality.

Petrushevskaya's portrayal of humanity alone and stripped of certainties clearly coincides with the world view of the theatre of the Absurd in western and central Europe. But as Martin Esslin points out, the same is true of French Existentialist theatre; it really only differs from Absurdism in the theatrical form it uses to make its point. While Existentialists present logical proofs of the world's absurdity '...the Theatre of the Absurd has renounced arguing *about* the absurdity of the human condition; it merely *presents* it in being – that is, in terms of concrete stage images'.[27] In a century characterized by disillusionment, this is the true test of a play's Absurdity, and Petrushevskaya's work contains many elements which can classify it alongside the works of Beckett, Ionesco and Pinter, despite the isolation of Soviet theatre from contemporary movements in the rest of Europe.

[25] Zonina, 495.
[26] Interview with Sigrid McLaughlin, quoted in *The Image of Women in Contemporary Soviet Fiction*, ed. Sigrid McLaughlin, Basingstoke, 1989, 98.
[27] Esslin, 25.

(A brief mention must be made here of the status of the Theatre of the Absurd in the USSR: neither the third edition of the *Bol'shaya Sovetskaya Entsiklopediya* nor the first edition of the *Teatral'naya Entsiklopediya* affords it an entry, but both list Beckett and Ionesco individually. Beckett is described as a 'representative of modernism',[28] whose plays 'express the spiritual crisis of the bourgeois intelligentsia in the West'.[29] Ionesco 'mocks contemporary philistines who are outwardly respectable but in essence worthless'.[30] No translations of their works are listed, although there are articles on 'the French avant-garde'. It would seem likely that Petrushevskaya at least knew of their work when she started writing plays: 'When I began to write plays, I rummaged through all sorts of drama, and *read all the foreign plays I could get my hands* on...'[31] (my italics). Performances of Absurdist works have in the past few years, with the advent of glasnost', become quite common in the USSR, especially in theatre-studios.)

One of the main criticisms levelled against Petrushevskaya by Soviet critics is that her plays deal almost exclusively with the pettiest *bytovoi* (everyday) aspects of Soviet life, that is, the grindingly monotonous daily round of living family life in material and spiritual poverty. Petrushevskaya describes the details and dialogue of modern Soviet life with an accuracy that has shaken even critics who dislike her subject matter and she has been described as 'a kind of feminist Chekhov'.[32] But to describe them as 'realist' is to disregard the elements of farce, surreality and meaningless nonsense that infiltrate into everyday life in these plays, and their inconclusive and seemingly shallow plot structures. Like Pinter's Absurd plays, Petrushevskaya's are 'more real than the realists' ', because they describe a different 'slice of life':

> ... the champions of social realism.... water down the reality of their picture of the world by presupposing that they have solutions for problems ... that may well be insoluble or by implying that it is possible to know the complete motivation of a character, or, above all, by presenting a slice of reality that is less essential, and hence less real, less true to life, than a theatre that has selected a more fundamental aspect of existence. If life in our time is basically absurd, then any dramatic representation of it that comes up with neat solutions and produces the illusion that it all 'makes sense', after all, is bound to contain an element

---

[28] *Bol'shaya Sovetskaya Entsiklopediya*, 3rd. edn., vol. 3, M., 1970, 98.

[29] *Teatral'naya Entsiklopediya,* vol 1, M., 1961, 488.

[30] *Teatral'naya Entsiklopediya,* vol 2, M., 1963, 889-90.

[31] Zonina, 495.

[32] For example, on the cover blurb of *Stars in the Morning Sky: Five New Plays from the Soviet Union*, introduced by Michael Glenny, London, 1989.

of oversimplification, to suppress essential factors, and reality expurgated and oversimplified becomes make-believe.[33]

Petrushevskaya refuses to write plays with neat solutions,[34] and her depiction of everyday reality is only the backdrop to the dramas of characters 'at the extreme edge of their living' which are going on all the while; although the plays are set in realistic locations, they also contain a different, and more essential 'slice of reality' which deals with more fundamental human questions, as is borne out by their style as much as their subject matter.

It is Petrushevskaya's longer plays (*Music Lessons* and *Three Girls in Blue*), which have almost traditional plots, that are nearest to being conventionally realist, but even these diverge from the realist canon in important respects. The characters in *Music Lessons* seem to be clearly defined – their full names, ages and relationships to each other are set out in the *dramatis personae*, and they seem initially to be conventional characters in a drama of bourgeois family life – the nosy neighbour, doting parents, errant son, etc. But each gradually changes as the play progresses: the neighbour, Anna Stepanovna, is bossy to the (poor) Gavrilovs, subservient to the Kozlovs; Nikolai goes from errant to dutiful; his father is revealed as a cruel man who almost destroyed his marriage, rather than the doting husband and father that he first appeared; Nina Gavrilova, who stands up for her rights in her own home, becomes the ideal fiancée that the Kozlovs want her to be – she hardly speaks, just takes orders, when she is taken in to their flat; and Nikolai's vulgar acquisitive girlfrlend Nadya is totally transformed – the Kozlovs barely recognise her when she comes to them for help, pregnant, having attempted to poison herself – the predator become prey.

In *Three Girls in Blue* too, characters are subject to a similar variability: Ira is initially a doting mother, then simply abandons her son; Svetlana is angry and unpleasant to Ira's son, until asked to look at him in her professional capacity as a doctor, when she is transformed (literally in the stage directions *preobrazhaetsya* (is transformed or transfigured)(158)) into a woman who cares far beyond the call of duty for her patient. Characters in the shorter plays are just as prone to volatility, for which there is seldom any obvious motive, and this has the effect of alienating the audience from the characters on stage. Since heroes and villains can so easily swap places, it becomes impossible to side with or judge characters, especially as the audience does not know *why* they change, and so Petrushevskaya achieves her aim of forcing the audience to look quite detachedly at the characters on stage, question their lives but at the same time remain humane – not judge characters or

---

[33] Esslin, 263.
[34] See note 10.

ask 'who is guilty?', but ask themselves 'why?', and hopefully recognize their own muddled, contradictory lives in the vacillations of the characters on stage.

Several of the shorter plays are peopled by characters without recognizable names, denoted only by letters or numbers (as in the plays *A Glass of Water, Isolation Ward* and *The Execution*), or generic descriptions (mother, son and guard in *Visiting Time*; doctor, major and driver in *The Execution*). Yet another, *Andante,* has characters whose names do not appear to make any sense – a man called Mai, and three women, Yulya, Bul'di and Au. These strange, confusing plays, all of them portrayals of the brutality of human life, are made more bewildering by the way that the characters' lack of identity (signified by their namelessness) dehumanizes them even further than their situation has already done. Once more, the effect on the audience is alienation – there are none of the symbols of identity that we usually cling to, and the characters seem slightly other than human.

A play which uses a similar effect to slightly different ends is *Columbine's Flat*, in which the three characters have the *commedia dell'arte* names Kolombina, Arlekin and P'ero. All are actors, but these are their real names, not stage roles – pantomime reality is transformed into the 'reality' of these characters' lives, and then further confused by P'ero and Kolombina rehearsing Shakespeare (Kolombina playing Romeo to P'ero's Juliette), and P'ero then being dressed up as a girl (the screen scene, another theatrical tradition, brought into 'real life') to avoid being discovered by Arlekin alone with his wife.

All these plays illustrate the same inconstancy of human character that Beckett recognized as a basic problem of human existence; that as character is constantly changed by the passage of time, self-knowledge and the attainment of one's desires are impossible since '... we are, at no single moment in our lives, identical with ourselves'.[35] Knowledge of others is equally impossible, since they are equally subject to change, and the concept of character loses the fixed meaning it has in realist works – and in part loses its relevance, since the idea of fixed individual characteristics is swept away, making a nameless, de-individualised figure (A.,1st Guard etc.) just as descriptive of the human condition as one who is provided wlth the identity of name and age which in fact tell us nothing.

Alongside the breakdown of character, Petrushevskaya's plays also display a distinct lack of the rational plot development vital to realism. In fact, many of them show very little plot development whatsoever, as M. Turovskaya points out: 'It is a peculiarity of the plot construction of Petrushevskaya's plays that the characters bring with them on to the stage a heap of their own human, all too human failings... but nothing ever seems to happen between them... The

---

[35] Esslin, 51.

exchange of words is often the most important thing that happens in them [the plays]'.[36]   Above all, these plays lack resolution – the judgement that Petrushevskaya refuses to pass on people. Some seem to go nowhere, merely circling round to return to their starting point, like *I'm a Sweden Fan:* the long-lost grandmother appears and tries to entice her grandson away with her, but leaves without even making contact with him; as the play ends, he is watching television, as unaffected by his grandmother's plight as he was at the start by his stepmother's.

Other plays are simply suspended: father and son in *A House and a Tree* seem to be on the verge of reconciling irreconcilable differences, when the real motivation behind the son coming home is revealed – his homeless friends want to move into his father's house – and the play stops in a *nemaya stsena* (dumb tableau) which recalls the final tableau of surprise in Gogol's *The Government Inspector (Revizor)*. (Such comparison with Gogol' is perhaps peculiarly apt, as both writers, while concentrating on the most mundane details, accept that bizarre, inexplicable and farcical events form part of daily life: a humble civil servant can become a phantom overcoat-ripper, while in Petrushevskaya's *Get up, Anchutka!*, a play in which the characters are brought together by the ins-and-outs of a Soviet apartment exchange, an old woman can be brought in to cast spells and eventually turn to dust before the assembled company, without anyone batting an eyelid. *The Overcoat (Shinel')* is apparently the subject of Petrushevskaya's second animated film scenario; the first was an award-winning animation, *The Tale of Tales (Skazka skazok)*).

Three Girls in Blue ends with a similar suspension, when Svetlana's mother-in-law, Leokadiya, silent up to this point, enters to declare, in a loud, clear voice, that the last sound roof in the house has started to leak: the effect is stunned silence not only because of the force with which Leokadiya suddenly speaks out, but because her announcement scuppers the resolution which the play had seemed to be building up to. Ira has returned to the dacha, purged of illusions, and all three girls seem determined to live in harmony – not a happy ending, but at least a *modus vivendi,* is in sight. That one more roof is leaking is yet another trial, a blow not only to morale but also to the sense of home and family which had momentarily seemed to be emerging. The optimistic mood of the final meditations in *Three Sisters* which helps the sisters to go on living despite what they have lost, is replaced in *Three Girls in Blue* by yet another misfortune, and whether the girls will cope without the life-line of belief in a better future is left unanswered by their silence at the end of the play. Leokadiya's statement and the effect that it produces could be said to negate everything that *Three Girls in Blue* seemed to be leading up to, real life denying the easy resolution of realism with a final twist, the *nemaya stsena* (dumb tableau) expressing man's lack of

---

[36] M. Turovskaya, 'Trudnye p'esy', *Novyi mir*, 1985, 12, 248-9.

solutions for the problems he faces and failure to cope with inexplicable reality.

The final twist plays a similar role in *Love*, where having established that they do not love one another, Sveta is suddenly persuaded by her mother's disapproval that marriage to Tolya is not such a bad thing after all; her mother is pleased to see them go, as she will have the flat to herself, rather than distraught at losing her daughter; so the natural logic of the words in the play – the couple parting – is negated by the actions the characters finally take.

Last words can not only negate a play's logic – in several cases, they deprive the play of any logic or meaning at all. The communication that had almost been established in *The Stairwell* breaks down as Slava and Yura leave, and their conversation becomes a set of garbled and meaningless promises to play a funeral march for Galya if she ever needs one:

Yura: Only, often, we can't, but when we can, then please, feel free. From time to time. (214)

With Yura's final words, a disconnected 'from time to time' with which he seems to be seeking to disassociate himself from Galya and his promises to her, the two leave, having lost touch with Galya.

A similar disconnection creeps into the final lines of *Smirnova's Birthday,* when the women's conversation is interrupted by the arrival of Valya from *Cinzano*, transformed for female company into Valentin, a 'young specialist' about to take a trip to Japan, who denies any knowledge of Pasha or Kostya (although he has obviously just come from *Cinzano,* bringing a bottle of the said drink with him). The coherence of theme that the women had achieved is destroyed by his arrival; Rita and Polina continue their family reminiscences, although Polina's anecdotes of Kostya's kindness and humanity are suddenly brought into contrast with what Valya knows about his condition at the end of *Cinzano,* and revealed as an illusion; Elya Smirnova and Valya, old friends, carry on a conversation as disjointed and meaningless to an outsider as the three men's conversation in *Cinzano*, and the play ends with Valya's words:

Valentin: Smirnova, what a good thing it is that there's you. (141)

What these words refer to – whether Valya is simply pleased to find somewhere to spend the night, or means something of great significance – is left unexplained. In both *The Stairwell* and *Smirnova's Birthday,* people approach true communication – but retreat at the last from meaning into the more comfortable non-communication that makes up everyday speech; rather than facing the realities that communicating can reveal, they slip back into the incoherence of life without either solutions or any real meaning.

If this is true of plays where characters approach understanding, then it is even more the case when completely farcical plays like *Columbine's Flat* and *The Parkbench-Prize* (*Skameika-premiya*) are involved: the pace of farce builds up through the plays and, rather than revealing a moral, they end in a frenzy of nonsense which is particularly ironic and absurd as both plays are set among workers of the Soviet theatre, that bastion of social and Socialist Realism. Ksyusha and Bakh are attempting to win a prize by writing a play about the morals of the working class, and the play's stilted, Soviet dialogue makes up much of the dialogue of *The Parkbench-Prize*. Unfortunately, the old Estonian, Al'ma Yanovna, with whom Ksyusha is sharing a room in a holiday home, speaks poor Russian and does not realize what they are doing; she takes the play's dialogue for genuine arguments between the couple, mis-hears everything that is said to her and seems to be carrying on a separate conversation from the others. The 'realist' play gradually becomes entwined with the meaningless, half-correct ramblings of Al'ma Yanovna, and conversation becomes so confused that Ksyusha and Bakh explain to the old lady that they are going to sit on a bench outside to write their hopefully prize-winning play – the *skameika-premiya* of the play's title, indicative of the level of coherence to which the 'realist' playwright has sunk by the end of the play.

The breakdown in plot structure – the lack of action and the lack of resolution that Petrushevskaya's plays display – sets them apart from the realist plays which they might seem to resemble in their concentration on the everyday, and in their accurate record of contemporary speech. But even the 'taperecorder effect', a term used by some Soviet critics to describe Petrushevskaya's writing,[37] although it would appear to be the apex of realist writing, in fact serves quite a different end. Turovskaya asserts that Petrushevskaya raises *zhargon* (slang, everyday speech) to the level of a literary phenomenon, and that this *zhargon* reveals a great deal about society:

> ...half-destroyed grammar and the breakdown of colloquial language make even the most educated speech seem strange and act as levellers among the characters. The corrosion of language is an indicator of the rise in the level of social entropy.[38]

The everyday has broken down – 'social entropy' has set in, not merely in the political sense of Brezhnevian *zastoi* (stagnation), but in a much more far-reaching sense; human society has fallen prey to entropy

---

[37] Quoted by Victoria Vainer, 'An Interview With Liudmila Petrushevskaya', *Theater* (Yale School of Drama), 3, 1989, 62.
[38] Turovskaya, 249.

('degradation or disorganisation') and absurdity[39] – and the accurate recording of everyday speech serves only to emphasize this. The fallibility of words as a method of communication has long been recognized, and Petrushevskaya's characters, living in a collapsing world, display the decay of language as they do the decay of social structures.

The most obvious instruments of man's failure to express himself in the modern world are the channels of mass-communication which he has set up to facilitate communication. Televisions blare in the suburban homes of *Music Lessons*, but they emit only explosions rather than any coherent commentary, and distract people's attention from one another, from conversation and, in the final scene, from moral responsibility for one's actions. Telephones fare no better – they either ring constantly and when answered go dead, as in *I'm a Sweden Fan* – or, as in *Three Girls in Blue*, the connection made between callers is purely technical. Ira's mother is first seen on the phone; we hear only her side of the conversation and her pleas not to be hung up on – it seems that she is no longer known at the office she is calling; and she finds herself having a conversation with the deaf husband of a friend she is trying to call. Ira's communication with her mother reaches its lowest ebb when they speak on the phone: she does nothing but lie, saying that she is at the dacha, when in fact she is in a seafront booth in Koktebel, and the emotional links between mother and daughter collapse – Ira's mother speaks 'without expression' (191) and says that she is going into hospital, leaving her grandson alone in the flat. Modern methods of communication seem to hinder human contact, rather than making it easier, and the presence of a physical barrier between two people trying to communicate seems to encourage them to lie and inflict pain on each other.

As is illustrated by the case of Ira and her mother, the closeness of a relationship is no guarantee of communication. Indeed, talk between friends is often so incomplete as to be almost incomprehensible: so much is taken as read in incomplete sentences, and allusion to past events plays such a role that conversation seems to be in code in plays like *Cinzano* where old friends exchange phrases that have built up over years of being together and slip into foreign languages and different characters as the mood takes them. In general, contemporary language as Petrushevskaya records it is far from dictionary Russian –

'Everyone speaks in a corrupted language – for example, a specialist in rare languages [Ira in *Three Girls in Blue*] forms the simplest Russian phrases with incorrect grammar.' [40]

---

[39] Defined as 'out of harmony with reason or propriety; incongruous, unreasonable, illogical', Esslin, 23.
[40] Malinkovich, 199.

– that is to say, close to Russian as it is actually spoken, with all the grammatical errors that exist as part of common usage. Sentences are compressed to their essence and the series of particles (*tak* (so), *nu* (well) etc.) that often pass for speech –

Valya: What, you don't live here?
Pasha: Temporarily.
Valya: You temporarily *do* live here, or temporarily don't?
Kostya: Today he does, that's all that matters.
Valya: But in general, where?
Pasha: Now still nowhere for a while already again. (*Cinzano*,107)

Pronunciation and stress are variables: 'pónyala': 'navernóe': 'voshche' for 'voobshche': 'shchas' for 'seichas': 'Iryn' for 'Irin': 'Ya tol'ko noch' nochuyú': 'yazýki' (all in *Three Girls in Blue*). People's conversations are filled with clichés and proverbs half-remembered and half-understood by those who hear them (Polina in *Smirnova's Birthday* is confused by the phrase *'voz'mite den'gi na royale'* ('take the money off the grand piano', which means, in essence, 'you can whistle for your money'): she keeps insisting that the family does not have a grand piano, only an upright (126)): aphorisms that should contain important truths have become platitudes and are used carelessly. Talk is full of non-sequiturs, as different people's trains of thought become entwined without actually coordinating: A., in *Isolation Ward*, is describing a visit to the cinema, whilst her companion B. is relating her daughter's sad life story, and in fact talking to her dead granddaughter; each is following her own obsession without listening; and many of the characters seem to be entirely deaf to their interlocutors, like Al'ma Yanovna in *The Parkbench-Prize*, who latches on to single words out of the context in which they are spoken and puts them into the context of her own knowledge – Bakh, the playwright in the play, is Bach the composer to her.

Occasionally, language breaks down completely, as happens in *Andante* and *The Parkbench-Prize*, where different languages are being spoken by the characters. Al'ma Yanovna cannot grasp the concepts of masculine and feminine nouns, the structure of tenses or the declension of Russian nouns, and her sentences become increasingly confused and meaningless:

Al'ma Yanovna: ... Ona, muzhchina, kogda nervnichaet, mozhet krichat' na zhena, chto ona ego ub'et. U menya byl muzh, Karl. Ona mne eto govorila. Nuzhno prosto perevesti razgovor na drugaya storona, o literatura, o pogoda. Zhenshchina umnyi, muzhchina glupaya.... (292)

The situation is even worse in *Andante*, where a family of returning diplomats speak an entirely different language to the woman renting their flat, Au; she *thinks* that she understands them and tries to speak the same language – only to realize that she is saying something quite other than she thinks. Not only is Au excluded from understanding – the language is incomprehensible to the audience too, and the final scenes of wild chanting and dancing seem like some exotic tribal ritual rather than goings-on in a Moscow flat.

The disintegration of language into nonsense which is visible in everyday conversation is highlighted when it falls into the hands of deliberate comics like the clowning duo, Slava and Yura in *The Stairwell*. The taciturn straight man, Slava, steps in to undermine Yura's extravagant, overdramatised statements:

> Yura: ... I love your little plaits of hair,
> All twined round like a basket there
> And I shall call you Zina-fair.
> That's a poem I wrote when I was ten years old.
> Galya: Was she your girlfriend?
> Yura: No, I just wrote it. She was the school nurse. But you can change it, you can put in Marina-fair or Irina-fair, as circumstances demand:
> I love your little plaits of hair
> All twined round like a basket there
> And I shall call you ... (*thinks*)
> Slava: Garlic-breath.
> Yura: I'll call you sweetly Galya-fair. (207)

The men perform a linguistic double act, backing each other up, changing the conversation's direction and pulling against each other, one excessively polite, the other overtly rude. Yet despite their clownishness, Slava and Yura perhaps come closest to expressing the true tragedy of the dislocation of the human condition. In fact, they resemble nothing more than 'holy fools' as they leave, accepting food and drink from Galya, asking her forgiveness and almost giving her their blessing. Although they play the fool, they touch more honestly, and with more genuine sympathy, on human isolation than almost any of Petrushevskaya's characters, and express the absurdity – and the tragedy – which lies behind every commonplace human action, as Pinter's characters do in his plays which are equally 'realistic' in their recording of speech, and equally significant beyond the bounds of realism:

> Everything is funny; the greatest earnestness is funny; even tragedy is funny. And I think what I try to do in my plays is to get to this recognizable reality of the absurdity of what we do and how we behave and how we speak...The point about tragedy is

28

that it is *no longer funny*. It is funny and then it becomes no longer funny.[41]

Petrushevskaya's use of contemporary language has the same results: human speech is shown up as comically inadequate and reveals the absurdity of all our attempts at communication, and the impossibility of really conveying what we mean to others, the tragedy which lies behind everyday absurdity.

Yet although words are so inadequate, all of these characters talk incessantly, whether anyone is listening or not – '... the exchange of words is often the most important thing that happens in them [the plays]'.[42] Rather than having dialogues, the participants in conversations often tell their own stories without listening, talking against each other rather than to each other; but even though they communicate nothing, they seem compelled to speak all the same. Like Beckett's characters, it is almost as though they fear the emptiness of silence – like Vladimir in *Waiting For Godot* their response to it is 'Say something!... *(in anguish)* Say anything at all!'[43] *Songs of the Twentieth Century,* a monologue, highlights man's compulsion to speak and tell stories in a similar fashion to *Krapp's Last Tape.* Krapp, listening to tapes he has made over the years, is moved by the lost love they recall and struck by the disintegration of the highflown dreams and style of his youth, which seem anathema to him now in his old age: 'Hard to believe I was ever that young whelp. The voice! Jesus! And the aspirations!..And the resolutions!'[44] His memories are victims of the constant change of human character – they no longer seem like his, so different is he now from the young man who made the tapes. The storyteller of *Songs of the Twentieth Century* is subject to the same process, speeded up and concentrated. At one sitting with his taperecorder, he plays many roles – the radio announcer, the poet, the football commentator, the future self who he dreams will be rich and successful; at one stage he is even himself for a moment:

>...There are pictures on the wall, 'Morning in the Pinewood'. What else.
>Aivazovskii: No. I'm talking to you, brothers and sisters, *I'm completely alone, I have nobody*, not one nor the other ... Moscow time is... (184, *Pesni*) (my italics)

But all these selves are ruthlessly rejected – he rewinds the tape, and starts again, telling a different story, being a different self:

[41] Interview with Hallam Tennyson, quoted by Esslin, 242.
[42] Turovskaya, 249.
[43] Samuel Beckett, *Waiting For Godot*, London, 1959, 63.
[44] *Krapp's Last Tape*, in *The Complete Dramatic Works of Samuel Beckett*, first edn., London, 1986, 218.

No. I'll start from the very beginning. Life starts from the beginning. Today is such and such a date, a new life. Every Monday, he starts a new life. (185, *Pesni*)

Like Krapp, he has a tale of lost love – in fact, love never even found, with a girl he once danced with – which he tries to recreate as a great romance on tape, only to rewind and admit that it never was.

This single figure, talking to himself and then obliterating his own words, is an eloquent expression of the human condition – both amusing and pitiable, constantly dissatisfied with his own dreams and constantly failing in them, trying desperately to find himself and make contact with others in the world, terrified by the loneliness of silence, yet unable to maintain communication with others or even himself. Language helps him evade the reality of human existence – the mutability of self, the unanswerable questions, the isolation – by filling up the silence, but does not in fact help him communicate with others or bring him nearer to understanding the truth. *A Glass of Water* portrays a similar situation: the woman who speaks most of the dialogue had two children who died as infants. She repeatedly returns to this subject, but each time she tells the story, the children have died in a different manner, and by providing so many different versions, she seems to be trying to control the pain of the story – she makes what really happened into fiction, thereby distancing herself from the agony of reality.

If anything, *talk* – whether to oneself or to others – is, as Pinter points out,

> ...a deliberate evasion of communication. Communication itself between people is so frightening that rather than do that there is continual cross-talk, a continual talking about other things, rather than what is at the root [of their relationship].[45]

Even alone, as *Songs of the Twentieth Century* shows, man avoids telling the truth or being himself, because to do so and face reality is so painful – as Ira in *Three Girls in Blue* and Galya in *The Stairwell* find out.

The words people use, then, are relatively weightless and slip easily into triteness and the *vran'e* (lying) that Petrushevskaya so hates and is attempting to expose. It is symbols and actions that are more likely to reveal truth:

> On the stage, language can be put into a contrapuntal relationship with action, the facts behind the language can be revealed....The concreteness and three-dimensional nature of the stage can be used

---

45 Interview with Kenneth Tynan, quoted by Esslin, 244.

to add new resources to language as an instrument of thought and exploration of being.[46]

Many of Petrushevskaya's plays have a poetic image – however cruel – that expresses more of the truth of the situation than any of the play's words: in *The Uncooked Joint, or, A meeting of Friends*, it is the raw leg of lamb remaining uncooked throughout the evening that tells the truth about the state of the couple's relations, rather than any of the words exchanged between the 'friends' who stand by as the husband beats the wife. Similarly in *Cinzano*, the chicken that Kostya's parents bring to lunch every weekend reveals everything about the family's disharmony:

> Kostya: They come to visit their grandchildren and bring a chicken with them. For eight people...Lunch is already ready without this chicken, we could've eaten long ago, but no, they must have it cooked. Everything gets cold. And they, stupid fools that they are, don't understand that all their charity just causes illwill. (116)

Symbols stand in contrast to the lies people would *like* to tell, just as many of their words are denied by their actions: the Kozlovs see themselves as generous benefactors to the less fortunate – but they still reject their son's pregnant girlfriend; Zyabreb, one of the characters in *Get Up, Anchutka!*, although he claims to be a rational man with every faith in doctors, still goes to a wise woman for a cure; Nikolai Ivanovich expresses his great passion for Ira in *Three Girls in Blue* not by some romantic gesture, but by having a privy built for her in the dacha garden, bringing their romance down to where it truly belongs – an exchange of goods.

But perhaps most significant as a measure of the lies being told, the meaninglessness of words being spoken, are the points at which action itself dissolves and unreality breaks in on everyday suburban life. *Music Lessons* is the play in which this occurs most startlingly, perhaps because it is the play that seems initially to be closest to the realist plot of a bourgeois family drama. But occasionally, the action suddenly takes on a quite different character. When Nikolai is asked to show off the results of his music lessons, and play the piano while his father sings, the falseness of the situation is revealed:

> *Nikolai sits down at the piano with a shrug. His father stands at his side. The influence of television is obvious. The father sings 'The Grey Dawn was Falling'. He sings tensing every nerve, not as one sings round the homecoming table, from the heart, but as*

---

[46] Esslin, 86.

people who have dreamed all their life of singing sing. Such singing does not normally produce a pleasant impression: on the contrary, everyone around the table averts their eyes.
(9/10)

When the song ends, Nikolai and Nadya dance to music on the radio – first the *Adagio* from *Swan Lake*, then Khachaturyan's *Sabre Dance*, then, when the news comes on, they dance to the text – all the time dancing on the spot. The Kozlovs' conventions become ridiculous when portrayed in such a stylized fashion, and all their fears of the common Nadya taking over their home are amplified as they are forced to accept her staying the night – she sits at their piano, playing *Chizhika-pyzhika (Chopsticks)*, whilst they arrange the room for her:

... Nadya plays Chopsticks. Kolya brings pillows out of grandmother's room ...grandmother runs in behind him. Taisa Petrovna takes fresh linen into grandmother's room. Everything happens exceptionally quickly, to the tune of Chopsticks, and suddenly grandmother appears in her nightdress, sitting on the couch... (13)

This almost silent-film-like hyperactivity makes Nadya seem all the more predatory to the Kozlovs – and their fears all the more laughable to the audience. But it is perhaps the tragic side of surreal action which is most effective in the play. By the end of the play, Nina has returned to her home, certain that Nikolai does not care for her, and the pregnant Nadya has been turned away by the family: all is seemingly peaceful in the Kozlov home, now they are rid of the girls who have become victims to their heartless morality, and they settle down to watch hockey on television. Then the mood changes: *'Everything that follows seems to the Kozlovs like an awful dream. All freeze'.*[47] Both girls reappear, lowered from the ceiling on swings, Nadya proffering her baby – it has been born without a head, she says, so they won't have to feed it; the family resolutely ignores them:

Taisa Petrovna: [the mother] ... Take no notice of them. If you take no notice of them, they'll leave us alone. (70)

But the swings lower relentlessly into the family's life, vivid symbols of the crimes on their consciences, forcing them to bend down as they walk until

---

[47] In the later collection of plays, only '*All freeze*' appears in the stage directions.

> *Nikolai buries his head deeper and deeper in the sofa, and freezes in an almost horizontal position, his knees drawn up to ward off the swooping swings.* (70)

The sudden shift from realism to dream-like symbolism reveals the truth that the family try to avoid by watching television – that their attempts to escape their moral responsibilities and live as before will be haunted by conscience. The strange and unexpected actions on the stage are more potent than any indignant verbal condemnation of the family could be, because rather than delivering a sermon, more appropriate to a Victorian melodrama than to the present century, they leave the audience with an impression of the family's inner discomposure – their knowledge of their own cowardice and hypocrisy.

In several plays, action becomes increasingly disjointed and surreal as the characters' words sink further and further into meaninglessness, as happens in *Andante*. At first the lodger, Au, believes that she understands the diplomats' language, and even strikes up some sort of relationship with Yulya, the diplomatic wife. But when the husband and his lover arrive to stay in the flat as well, any sympathy that might have been felt for Au is pushed aside; they deliberately speak their incomprehensible language, threaten her with the police and pour scorn on her pleas. Then the diplomats take the mysterious 'tablets' that they have brought back from abroad, and undergo a complete change of personality. In some sort of narcotic frenzy, they turn their attention to Au, promising her their affection and any gifts she might want; meanwhile, their speech becomes increasingly senseless, a series of barely connected exclamations, until they all turn to Au, with the words

> *All*: Poor thing, she's raving...Our little pipette...come to us, we'll sing a song in four parts!
> *They perform a round dance.* (243)

The manic chanting and *khorovod* (round dance) on which the play ends express the total breakdown of communication; their selves completely changed by the 'tablets', these seemingly civilized modern Soviet people are reduced to an almost primaeval level which communicates nothing; they become truly absurd in every sense – ridiculous, illogical, purposeless – when neither speech nor actions any longer serve to convey meaning. Perhaps, freed from social constraint by the 'tablets' they take, these Soviet diplomats reveal the senseless activity that lies below the surface of society's brutal niceties and assumed rationality.

Petrushevskaya's plays are sometimes quite terrifying portrayals of decay – the breakdown of concrete surroundings, of the social fabric, of human relations and human communication: they are at times blackly funny, and at times horrifying in the brutality they describe. But their concern is not primarily social criticism, although to portray Soviet society of the Brezhnev years accurately is, surely, to compare the reality unfavourably with the propaganda. Petrushevskaya's concern is with individuals and their inability to face up to their own moral and spiritual situation:

Why do people, knowing all they do, live like that all the same?[48]

Her aim is to bring people to question the hollow standards by which they live and, above all, to tell the truth. To do so is to accept emptiness – Tolya's 'nothing' in *Love* – to stand at the edge of human existence, face one's fear and incomprehension and try to make real contact with others, rather than hiding behind the false values and false communication that hold a crumbling society together. Petrushevskaya writes with brutal accuracy, combined with deep sympathy for the hopeless people she portrays and understanding of human absurdity in an age without faith. The stagnation and decay of the society she depicts is the perfect setting for the cathartic realization of the rootlessness and senselessness that are usually hidden by convention, and Petrushevskaya has the resolute honesty needed to try to bring her characters – and her audience – to face the absurdity of man's position in the period of stagnation.

---

[48] Zonina, 495.

34

Bibliography

M. = Moscow

Primary Play Texts

Beckett, Samuel, *The Complete Dramatic works of Samuel Beckett,* 1st edn., London, 1986.

Beckett, Samuel, *Waiting For Godot,* London, 1959.

Chekhov, Anton, *P'esy,* Kiev, 1983.

Ionesco, Eugene, *Three Plays*, eds. H. F. Brookes and C. E. Fraenkel, London, 1965.

Petrushevskaya, Lyudmila, *Pesni XX veka: p'esy*, M., 1988.

Petrushevskaya, Lyudmila, *Tri devushki v golubom,* M., 1989.

Secondary Literature

Berlin, Isaiah, 'The State of Europe: Christmas Eve, 1989', *Granta,* 30, 1990, 148–50.

Bol'shaya Sovetskaya Entsiklopediya, 3rd edn., Vol 3, M., 1970, 98.

Clark, Katerina, 'The Centrality of Rural Themes in Postwar Soviet Fiction', in *Perspectives on Literature and Society in Eastern and Western Europe,* eds. Geoffrey A. Hosking and George F. Cushing, London, 1989, 76–100.

Esslin, Martin, *The Theatre of the Absurd*, 3rd edn., London, 1980.

Gershkovich, Aleksandr, *Teatr na Taganke (1964-1984)*, Benson, Vermont, 1986, 229.

Gessen, Elena, 'Kto boitsya Lyudmily Petrushevskoi?', *Vremya i my,* 81, 1984, 109–19.

Gessen, Elena, 'Pobeg iz sotsrealizma', *Strana i mir*, 6[54], 1989, 174–81.

Glenny, Michael, ed., *Stars in the Morning Sky: Five New Plays from the Soviet Union*, London, 1989.

Graffy, Julian and Geoffrey A. Hosking, eds., *Culture and the Media in the USSR Today*, London, 1989.

Kazak, Wolfgang, *Entsiklopedicheskii slovar' russkoi literatury s 1917 goda,* London, 1988, 596–7.

Laird, Sally, 'Soviet Literature – What Has Changed?', *Index on Censorship,* 7, 1987, 8–13.

Lowe, David, *Russian Writing since 1953: A Critical Survey,* New York, 1987, 195–200.

Malinkovich, Vladimir, 'Sostradanie (o p'esakh Lyudmily Petrushevskoi)', *Forum,* 16, 1987, 197–204.

McLaughlin, Sigrid, ed. and tr., *The Image of Women in Contemporary Soviet Fiction*, Basingstoke, 1989.

Sorokin, V., *The Queue,* tr. Sally Laird, New York and London, 1988.

Teatral'naya Entsiklopediya, 1st edn., M., Vol 1, 1961, 488; Vol 2, 1963, 889–90.

Turovskaya, M., 'Trudnye p'esy', *Novyi mir,* 12, 1985, 247-52.

Vainer, Victoria, 'An Interview wlth Liudmila Petrushevskaya', *Theater* (Yale School of Drama), 3, 1989, 61–4.

Voinovich, Vladimir, *Ivan'kiada*, Ann Arbor, 1976.

Vladimov, Georgii, *Tri minuty molchaniya,* Frankfurt, 1982.

Zonina, M., 'Bessmertnaya lyubov'', *Literaturnaya gazeta,* 47, 23 November 1983, 495.